OCEANS ALIVE

Jellyfish

by Ann Herriges

BELLWETHER MEDIA • MINNEAPOLIS, MN

Note to Librarians, Teachers, and Parents:

Blastoff! Readers are carefully developed by literacy experts and combine standards-based content with developmentally appropriate text.

Level 1 provides the most support through repetition of high-frequency words, light text, predictable sentence patterns, and strong visual support.

Level 2 offers early readers a bit more challenge through varied simple sentences, increased text load, and less repetition of high-frequency words.

Level 3 advances early-fluent readers toward fluency through increased text and concept load, less reliance on visuals, longer sentences, and more literary language.

Whichever book is right for your reader, Blastoff! Readers are the perfect books to build confidence and encourage a love of reading that will last a lifetime!

This edition first published in 2007 by Bellwether Media.

No part of this publication may be reproduced in whole or in part without written permission of the publisher. For information regarding permission, write to Bellwether Media Inc., Attention: Permissions Department, Post Office Box 1C, Minnetonka, MN 55345-9998.

Library of Congress Cataloging-in-Publication Data
Herriges, Ann.
  Jellyfish / by Ann Herriges.
     p. cm. — (Oceans alive!) (Blastoff! readers)
Summary: "Simple text and supportive images introduce beginning readers to jellyfish. Intended for students in kindergarten through third grade."
  Includes bibliographical references and index.
  ISBN-10: 1-60014-018-1 (hardcover : alk. paper)
  ISBN-13: 978-1-60014-018-1 (hardcover : alk. paper)
  1. Jellyfishes—Juvenile literature. I. Title. II. Series. III. Series: Blastoff! readers

QL377.S4H47 2007
593.5'3—dc22   2006000609

Text copyright © 2007 by Bellwether Media.
Printed in the United States of America.

Table of Contents

Jellyfish live in oceans all over the world.

4

Jellyfish travel in groups.
A group of jellyfish is
called a **smack**.

5

Some jellyfish live at the top
of the ocean.

Some jellyfish live deep in the ocean.

Most jellyfish are shaped like open umbrellas.

Their bodies are smooth
and **squishy**.

Jellyfish do not have eyes,
a brain, a heart, or bones.

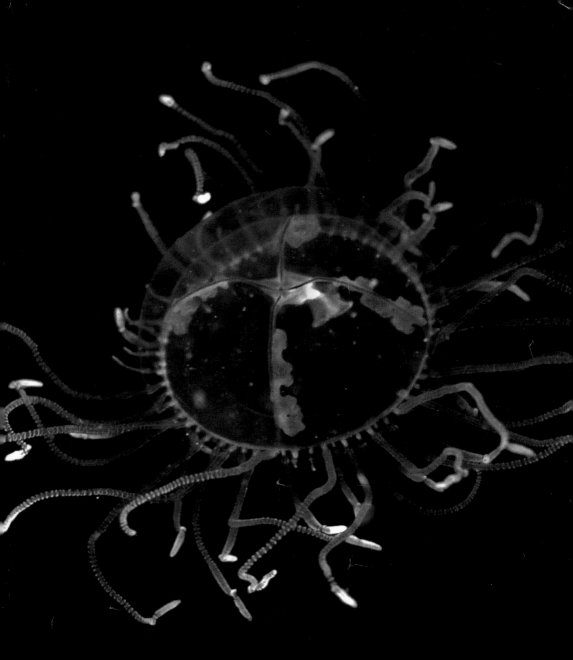

A jellyfish's body is
mostly water.

Jellyfish can be purple, pink, orange, and other colors.

Some jellyfish are no color at all.

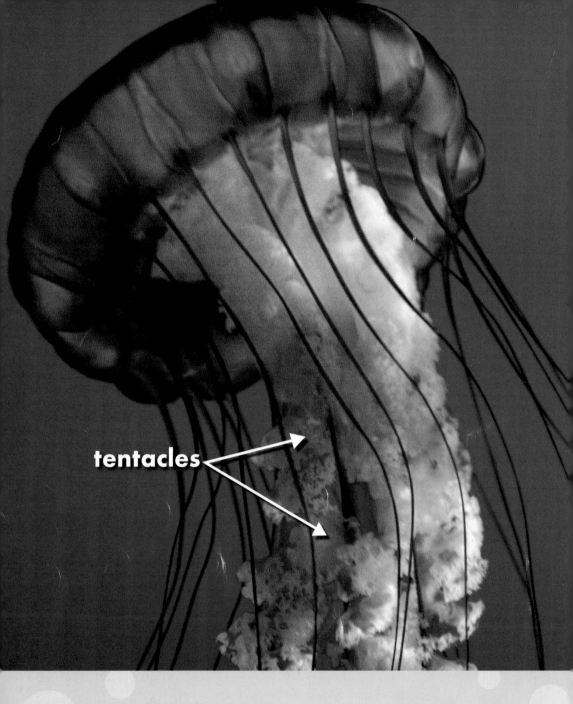

tentacles

Jellyfish have arms called **tentacles**. Tentacles can be short or long.

A jellyfish spreads out its
tentacles to search for food.

15

The tentacles have **stinging cells** that catch food.

The jellyfish brings the food
to its mouth.

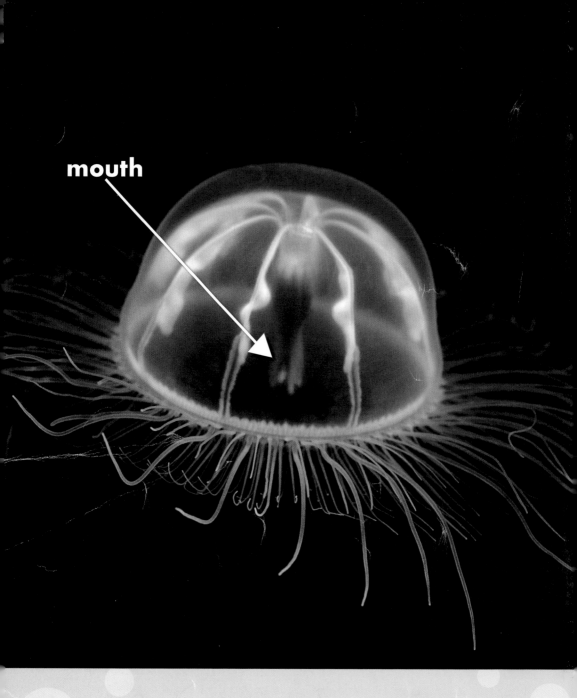

mouth

The mouth is a short **tube** that hangs down from the body.

feeding arms

Most jellyfish also have curly
feeding arms around
the mouth.

Jellyfish **squeeze** water through their bodies to swim. But they do not swim fast.

Jellyfish are **drifters**. They go wherever the ocean **current** takes them.

Glossary

current—the movement of water in the ocean; some currents are like rivers that flow through the ocean.

drifter—to move without any sense of purpose; instead of swimming, jellyfish travel by drifting in the ocean currents.

smack—a large group of jellyfish that drift together in the ocean; another name for a group of jellyfish is a brood.

squeeze—to force something through a space; jellyfish push water through their bodies to move themselves forward.

squishy—soft and wet

stinging cell—a part on a jellyfish's tentacle that pushes a stinger into a fish or other prey; the stinger shoots poison into the prey.

tentacles—the arms of some animals that are used for grabbing

tube—a long, hollow shape; a tube is shaped like a straw or a pipe.

To Learn More

AT THE LIBRARY

Andreae, Giles. *Commotion in the Ocean*. Wilton, Conn.: Tiger Tales, 2002.

Cash, Megan Montague. *I Saw the Sea and the Sea Saw Me*. New York: Viking, 2001.

George, Twig C. *Jellies: The Life of Jellyfish*. Brookfield, Conn.: Millbrook Press, 2000.

Landau, Elaine. *Jellyfish*. New York: Children's Press, 1999.

Schaefer, Lola M. *Jellyfish*. Chicago: Heinemann, 2002.

Tate, Suzanne. *Jenny Jellyfish: A Tale of Wiggly Jellies*. Nags Head, N.C.: Nags Head Art, 2001.

ON THE WEB

Learning more about jellyfish is as easy as 1, 2, 3.

1. Go to www.factsurfer.com

2. Enter "jellyfish" into search box.

3. Click the "Surf" button and you will see a list of related web sites.

With factsurfer.com, finding more information is just a click away.

Index

The photographs in this book are reproduced through the courtesy of: Lee Foster/Getty Images, front cover; Paul Nicklen/National Geographic/Getty Images, pp. 4-5, Tarik Tinazay/AFP/ Getty Images, p. 6; Bill Curtsinger/National Geographic/Getty Images, pp. 7, 8, 18; Stephen Frink Collection/Alamy, p. 9; Stock Connection/Alamy, p. 10; David Fleetham/Alamy, pp. 11, 19; Tore Hagman/Alamy, p. 12; Reinhard Dirscherl/Alamy, p. 13; William Eckersley/Alamy, p. 14; Gary Bell/Getty Images, p. 15; David Doubilet/Getty Images, pp. 16-17, 17(inset); Pete Atkinson/Getty Images, p. 20; Juan Martinez, p. 21.